Easy
To Use
Puppet
Shows

An effective teaching tool to use for ages 3-7

Joy Rothdiener

1stBooks – rev. 06/07/02

To Kaylie, Braden and the

many young Head Start children

that have touched

my life.

Preface

Easy to Use Puppet Shows is a collection of many puppet shows written over the course of my 12 years as a Head Start teacher. I have always loved seeing children's faces light up when they see a puppet. Puppets truly make a story come alive.

I have never met a child who didn't get excited to see a puppet. One day, as I struggled with a lesson plan on "Feelings and Emotions," I was motivated to write "Freddy Frog's Feelings." We presented it to the children as they sat spellbound. When we finished, the children said, "Do it again." The staff was also enthusiastic and excited.

Soon, we presented this puppet show at a parent meeting. What a winner it was! Not long after, I taught an early childhood class at Southwest Baptist University. We again featured "Freddie Frog's Feelings." The university students also were complimentary and offered many positive remarks. At that point, I realized that this puppet show had become an essential, helpful tool in our classroom.

So it began... Taking common lesson plan themes, I would write a puppet show. The staff and children began to look forward to the puppet shows. They would ask for another one.

Through the encouragement of my wonderful staff at Bolivar 1 Head Start, I compiled this collection of our favorite shows through the years. I hope you enjoy using them as much as I have enjoyed preparing them. Have fun!

Acknowledgments

I would like to thank the following people for their contribution to this book:

Chris Perstrope for the art work

Burton and Sylvia Murdock who provided valuable insights and much wisdom

John Rothdiener, Jodie McCrickard, Penni Cole and Jeanie Cunnyngham for their encouragement, patience, and kind words

To my many friends at OACAC Head Start that encouraged me to move forward on this project

The many young Head Start children that have inspired me to write this book.

Contents

Introduction

Easy To Use Puppet Shows is a valuable resource designed to:

- Help teachers gain confidence with puppets in the child's classroom
- Teach young children important learning concepts
- Be a time saver for busy teachers
- Be a tool that teachers will use repeatedly—bringing to life puppets through common lesson plan themes
- Make a teacher see the many benefits of puppets

Many teachers feel intimidated with puppets. Yet puppets are one of the most beneficial tools to own in the early childhood classroom. Puppets are a visual device that can bring a story to life and capture each child's attention—many times when all else seems to fail.

Each puppet show in this book is filled with important educational information for the young child. Children love to learn through puppets, which seem to make a story come alive.

The puppet shows in this book can be done with a minimal amount of rehearsal. You may want to repeat the story a few days later—kids absorb more each time they see a puppet show.

Puppets

Many puppets are brought to life in this book. If you do not own the puppets in this book, that's okay—this book is still for you. You may substitute some of the characters with the puppets you have or make a simple clip art puppet. You can easily color the patterns in this book, cut them out, laminate, and glue them on a craft stick. Over a period of time perhaps you can budget for puppets and begin to build your own collection. Some of the puppets in the shows are frequently used, some less frequently. However, you will most likely want to do these shows repeatedly, making it worthwhile to invest in puppets.

Puppet Stage

If you do not have a puppet stage available it is easy to improvise. You can use a large box or table with material or a sheet draped over it. Another idea is a tension curtain rod, with a curtain—set in a hallway. Be creative.

Scripts

Rehearse the script, so the puppeteers are comfortable with the puppet show. It may be beneficial for you to attach the script onto the back of the stage, making it possible for all the puppeteers to see the words. You might like to tape record the script ahead of time and have the puppets "lip-sync" the words. This can help if you are uncomfortable with puppets.

Additional Tips:

Be creative with your voices; practice them ahead of time. Make them funny and distinct. Put emotion into it.

Make the puppet that is talking move so that the children know who is saying the words. The action of the puppets captures the attention of the children.

Practice in front of a mirror. You can see the motions that best fit the puppet.

Have fun with it! Puppets are a wonderful way to release creativity. Make them come alive! As you practice you will find yourself more comfortable with doing puppet shows. You will see it as an essential tool, just as the kids will.

Feedback Time

These are ideas to stimulate conversation with the children. You can also use your own questions. Listen to the children as they share what they have learned and their own ideas.

Discuss the most important educational thoughts. Repetition is important at this age. Let the children retell the story back to you. Let them be creative as they tell the story. Encourage feedback from all the children, making sure not to put a child on the spot. Praise them for their answers and their effort.

Let's Be Healthy

Characters: Mother, Father, and Child (Abby)

SCRIPT

(Mother, Father, and Abby are in place)

Abby: (Sounding agitated) I don't like my vegetables. I won't eat them at dinner tonight or ever again.

Mother: Abby, I understand there are certain foods you like better than others. We all like different things. But one thing I know for certain is—it's important to eat nourishing foods to stay healthy.

Father: Yes, and vegetables are healthy.

Mother: So are fruit and milk. Our bodies need vitamins and minerals these foods provide.

Father: They help us to have strong bones and muscles. They also give us energy, which makes us feel better.

Abby: Why is that important?

Father: We only get one body and it's important to take care of that body.

Abby: Okay, I know it's good to eat healthy. Are there other ways to help take good care of my body?

Mother: Oh yes, Abby. There are many things you can do to help stay healthy. One thing is to get to bed early so your body can get the sleep it needs.

Father: And exercise. It's important to exercise our muscles; it's great to be in good shape.

Mother: Did you know that you even need sunshine? Sunshine gives us Vitamin D, which helps our bones and our teeth? It also makes us feel better. But when you go outside, don't forget the sunscreen. You always should protect your skin from the sun.

Abby: I didn't know all that stuff. Is there anything else I need to know to be healthy?

Father: There sure is, Abby. It's important to stay clean.

Mother: That means taking baths or showers often, and using soap to scrub yourself clean. Shampoo your hair well, too. Don't forget to wash behind your ears.

Father: Remember to wash your hands often—especially after going to the bathroom, blowing your nose, coughing, sneezing, handling pets, and before you eat. Clean the top and the bottom of your hands and between your fingers, too. Make sure you use soap and warm water.

Mother: Do you know what else needs to be cleaned?

Abby: What, Mother?

Mother: Your teeth. You should brush your teeth at least two times a day. It is also important to visit a dentist regularly. They can help you keep your teeth healthy.

Abby: There is a lot to remember to stay healthy.

Father: Yes, and don't forget to dress warm when it's cold outside. You should wear a warm coat, hat, and gloves.

Mother: And you should always wear shoes, especially when you go outside, so you don't hurt your feet.

Abby: I will try to be careful. But what would happen if I did hurt myself?

Mother: Sometimes we need to wash the sore spot and put a band-aid on. Other times we might have to take you to the doctor, honey. Doctors are there to help people feel better. Sometimes people get sick or hurt and they need to go to a doctor's office or a hospital. They may need a bandage, or medicine…

Father: Or a shot.

Abby: Ouch! I guess it would be okay to have a shot if it prevents me from getting sick—or helps me to get well.

Mother: Abby, sometimes accidents happen. That's when Doctor's and nurses can help us. But there are things we can do to help. Do you remember them?

Abby: (Seems to be thinking) I need to get enough sleep, exercise and sunshine. I also need to keep my body clean. I need to wash my hands often, with warm water and soap. I should brush my teeth at least two times a day. I should dress warm when it's cold and always wear shoes. I think that's all.

Mother: No it isn't, Abby. You forgot one important thing, silly!

Abby: Oh yes, I guess I will eat all my vegetables tonight. I do want a healthy body. So right now, I am going to go play in the sunshine. Better get that sunscreen on. Bye.

Feedback:

- Why should we eat healthy foods?

- What other things can we do to help us stay healthy?

- When should we wash our hands?

- How often should we brush our teeth?

- How should we dress when it's cold outside?

- How do doctors help us?

Joy Rothdiener

Summer Safety

Characters: Boy puppet (Brian) and girl puppet (Abby)

SCRIPT

(Brian and Abby in place)

Abby: (Whistling part of "You are My Sunshine")

Brian: (interrupts) Yippee! Hi Abby! School is out and summer is here—what are your plans?

Abby: I love summer, Brian. It gets really hot but it is so much fun to cool off in the pool. I never go without an adult. I want to stay safe.

Brian: Great idea, Abby. I want you to be safe, too. What other plans do you have?

Abby: I am going to play outside, a lot.

Brian: We need to make sure we remind our moms of our sunscreen when we go outdoors. Or else we could get a nasty sunburn. Ouch! We should always protect our skin.

Abby: Yes, that's right, Brian. I am going to ride my bike this summer, too. Yes, with a helmet, Brian.

Brian: Good, Abby. You will remember not to play in the street, won't you?

Abby: Yes, I will. What are your plans this summer, Brian?

Brian: Mom says we will go on a vacation somewhere—maybe a beach.

Abby: That will be so much fun. We're taking some day trips; places like the zoo and amusement park. We are going to the County Fair, too. Mom is going to bake her yummy apple pie and enter it in the contest. She hopes to win a blue ribbon.

Brian: That will be a blast, Abby. I really like summer—everything seems so much more relaxed.

Abby: (Chuckling) Even my bedtime! Mom lets me stay up later at night since I don't have to get up for school in the morning. I love to play outside in the dark. I enjoy watching the lightning bugs and listening to the frogs croak.

Brian: I made up a song about summer. You might know it. It goes like this. (Sing to the tune of "You are My Sunshine")

(Brian and Abby both sing)

> *It is summer; the days are longer;*
>
> *I like to play outside all day.*
>
> *I like to swim and take vacation;*
>
> *I hope it never goes away.*

Abby: Let's climb a tree, Brian. I'll race you!

Brian: Okay. I'm on my way.

Feedback:

- What is the girl's name?

- What does Abby like to do when it gets real hot?

- What is the boy's name?

- How will they stay safe in the summer?

- What is Abby's mom going to bake for the fair?

- What do you like to do in summer?

What Makes Us Special

Characters: Polly Parrot, Freddy Frog, Rhonda Robin, Helen Hen, and baby bird (Optional)

SCRIPT

Polly Parrot: (sing to the tune of "London Bridge") *Hey listen, have you heard—I'm so glad that I'm a bird. I soar in the...*

Freddy Frog: (interrupts) Excuse me, Polly Parrot, what are you singing?

Polly Parrot: I wrote a song, Freddy.

Freddy Frog: Oh really. I didn't mean to interrupt. Will you sing it for me, please?

Polly Parrot: Okay, it goes like this. (Same tune as above)

Hey listen, have you heard?
I'm so glad that I'm a bird.
I soar in the sky,
And go so very high.

I eat worms and bugs and things;

I make a chirp and I sing;

I'm so glad I am a bird.

I hope you all have heard.

Freddy Frog: Wow! That is a neat song, Polly Parrot. I think I will write a song about me.

(Same tune as above)

I'm so glad I am a frog

Sit on lily pads and logs

Polly Parrot: (interrupts) Wait, Freddy. I am singing because I am a bird. You can't sing; you're a frog.

Freddy Frog: Polly, that's what you think. Listen. "Ribbit, ribbit."

Polly Parrot: That's not a song, Freddy. That's a croak.

Freddy Frog: What makes you so different from me?

Polly Parrot: For one thing I can lay eggs. Can you?

Freddy Frog: Yes. Frogs lay eggs, hundreds of them. They are very tiny. They hatch into little fish, then tadpoles, and then big frogs like me.

Polly Parrot: No, not that kind of eggs. I mean the kind with a shell.

Helen Hen: (clucking) We hens know all about laying eggs. Cluck, cluck. Did you know that I am a bird, too?

Polly Parrot: Yes, you are, Helen Hen. I am telling Freddy Frog what makes us birds sooooo special, Helen Hen.

Helen Hen: Did you tell him we have wings and that makes us able to fly?

Freddy Frog: Wow, that would be neat to be able to fly way up high. Seems like all I can do is hop from one lily pad to the next.

Polly Parrot: We can't hop like you Freddy, but we can soar through the skies because of our wings.

Rhonda Robin: (Flies in) Hey, you critters, watch me fly. (Demonstrate flying) I overheard you talking about why us birds are special. It's because we have beautiful feathers.

Freddy Frog: Hi, Rhonda Robin. It's true, I don't have feathers but I have slippery, slimy skin. I think that's pretty wonderful too.

Rhonda Robin: Yes it is, Freddy. I have to look for a worm to feed my little ones. Bye. (Flies off)

Freddy Frog: Is there anything else that makes you so special? (A bit sarcastically)

Polly Parrot: Yes, we have this thing called a beak. See.

(Freddy looks closely at beak)

Freddy Frog: Wow, a beak. (Appears to be thinking) I just have a nose and a mouth. I guess birds are special. (Pause, then excitedly) Hey, I know something I can do better!

Polly Parrot: What?

Freddy Frog: I can swim—watch me. (Dives out of sight for a few seconds then reappears)

Polly Parrot: That's true, Freddy. I like a birdbath or puddle every so often, but I can't swim like you. I think we are all special and different. Just like our friends sitting out there, they all look different and very special. I am glad we are all different or this would be a boring world. I know a song about this. Sing with me. (To the tune of "Frere Jacques")

I am special, I am special;
In the mirror you will see,
Someone very special, someone very special,
Look at me—you will see.

Feedback:

- What was the parrot's name?

- What was the frog's name?

- Why did Polly Parrot think birds were special?

- Why did Rhonda Robin have to leave in a hurry?

- Was Freddy Frog special, too?

- Are we special? Why?

Fall Fun

Characters: Squeaky Squirrel, Barbara Bear, Girl Puppet, (Abby) and Boy Puppet (Brian)

SCRIPT

(Squeaky Squirrel standing alone)

Squeaky Squirrel: (Sing to the tune of "Frere Jacques")

It is fall, It is fall;

Look and see, look and see.

All the pretty leaves,

Falling off the trees.

You will see, look and see.

(Barbara Bear appears)

Barbara Bear: What are you doing, Squeaky Squirrel?

Squeaky Squirrel: I made up a song about my favorite time of the year—fall. Another name for it is autumn.

Barbara Bear: I love fall, too. I am very busy in fall. I eat, and eat, and eat. Then I go to sleep for a long winter's nap. They say I hibernate, kind of a big word—for my long snooze. Better go. I must get busy. I have so much to do.

(Barbara Bear leaves)

Squeaky Squirrel: I better get busy, too. No time for singing. I need to hunt for nuts and acorns to put away in my secret hiding place for winter. They sure taste good when the ground is covered with snow. If it weren't for all my stored up food I'd go hungry. (Squeaky Squirrel leaves singing "It is Fall," as before)

(Brian and Abby appear)

Abby: I love fall, Brian, because of the changing leaves on the trees.

Brian: Yes, the trees are beautiful. I see orange, red, yellow, brown and green leaves. It is soooo colorful!

Abby: Brrr. It's getting chilly out here.

Brian: That's what happens in fall, Abby. The days start getting shorter and the temperatures start dropping.

Abby: And I can sure feel it. Brrr. What do you like to do in fall, Brian?

Brian: I like to play football with my friends. What do you like to do?

Abby: I like to visit the Pumpkin Patch.

Brian: I would love to see all those pumpkins.

Abby: It's neat to see how big some of those pumpkins get. I saw real small ones, too. Some are funny shaped and some are perfectly round. There are a lot of them. The man takes us on a hayride so we can pick out a special pumpkin to take home. It is really fun.

Brian: That makes me think of the hayride we go on in the fall. When we're done, we build a campfire and roast marshmallows.

Abby: Yummy! Maybe we can do that together sometime. But now we better get a jacket. Bye.

Brian: Goodbye everybody!

Feedback:

- What is another word for fall?

- What do bears do in the fall?

- What did Squeaky Squirrel do to get ready for fall?

- Name some things that Brian and Abby like to do in fall.

- What do you like to do in fall?

- What happens to trees in fall?

- Does the temperature feel different in fall?

Animal Friends

Characters: Polly Parrot, Donald Dog, Katie Cat, Melinda Horse, and Sassy Snake

SCRIPT

(Polly Parrot alone in scene)

Polly Parrot: Polly want a cracker? Polly want a cracker? Polly want a ...

Katie Cat: (Interrupts) Polly, go get a cracker so I can have some peace and quiet. Can't you please say something different than (sarcastically) Polly want a cracker?

Polly Parrot: I'm talking like parrots talk. I am trying to be a good pet. Polly want a cracker? Polly want a cracker?

Katie Cat: I'm a good pet, too, Polly. When my owners come home I run and greet them with a loud purr. When cats purr it means they're happy.

(Donald Dog appears, barking)

Donald Dog: I heard you talking. I know about being a good pet. When strangers come, I bark and scare them away. (Growls) I can sound tough and scary. I'm not mean. I 'm just being a good pet, protecting my owners. Other times I am very kind. I play ball with my owners. Sometimes, I chase the ball but don't always like to bring it back to them. Then they speak my name loudly, so I bring the ball to them. I want to make them happy. My owners take good care of me so I do my best for them.

(Melinda Horse appears)

Melinda Horse: Neigh, neigh. I'm a pet too, you know. I can't live in a house like you, because I'm too big. But I am helpful in other ways. I give people rides on my back. Neigh, neigh.

(Sassy Snake appears)

Sassy Snake: What about me?

Katie Cat: (Sounding unsure) Are you a pet too, Sassy Snake?

Sassy Snake: Yes, I am for some people. There are many different types of pets, you know. There are monkeys, lizards, fish, ferrets, hamsters, mice and many more.

Donald Dog: I didn't know there were so many types of pets.

Melinda Horse: Yes, and there is one thing we all have in common.

Polly Parrot: What's that, Melinda?

Melinda Horse: We all have needs. We need food and fresh water every day.

Polly Parrot: And we need people to spend time with us. We need to exercise to stay healthy.

(All the pets show agreement)

Katie Cat: And most of all, we need lots of T.L.C.

Polly Parrot: Katie Cat, what is T.L.C.?

Katie Cat: It means tender loving care.

Polly Parrot: Yes, we do need that. I better get busy working on my line again. Polly want a cracker?

(At this point all the pets agree it's time to go and say "Bye.")

Feedback:

- What was the parrot's name?

- What was Polly Parrot saying? Why?

- What does Donald Dog do?

- Can you name some other types of pets?

- What needs do pets have?

Freddy Frog's Feelings

Characters: Freddy Frog, Suzie Frog, Melody Turtle, Sammy Spider, and Marvin Mouse

SCRIPT

(Freddy Frog alone in scene)

Freddy Frog: (Freddy Frog is looking bored, humming softly) I'm bored. There's nothing to do today. Ho hum.

(Marvin Mouse appears)

Freddy Frog: There's my friend Marvin Mouse. Maybe he will play with me. Hey, Marvin, will you play with me? I am looking for someone to play with. Please.

Marvin Mouse: Sorry, Freddy. My mom says that I need to come right home today. We're going to the zoo.

Freddy Frog: Wow, you're really lucky to go to the zoo. I am not doing anything today. Hint, hint.

Marvin Mouse: Bye, Freddy, I've got to run. (He leaves)

23

Freddy Frog: (Alone, looking depressed) I would love to visit the zoo. I think I should be the one leaving for the zoo. I think I feel jealous of Marvin. It doesn't seem fair.

Melody Turtle: (As Freddy Frog is feeling sorry for himself, Melody Turtle sneaks up on him) What are you doing, Freddy?

Freddy Frog: (Startled, Freddy jumps) Wow, you surprised me, Melody Turtle. I am feeling kind of bored today. Nobody will play with me. (Sarcastically) Marvin Mouse is going to the zoo and I feel kind of jealous because he didn't ask me to go. I love the zoo. Do you want to play with me?

Melody Turtle: No way, Freddy. I am going to Alvin Alligator's house to play with him. Bye, Freddy.

Freddy Frog: (Sounding angry) Bye. Now I am really mad. I didn't want to play with those guys anyway.

Sammy Spider: (Crawls in)

Freddie Frog: Hey, Sammy. What are you doing?

Sammy Spider: I am feeling very hungry so I am looking for a bug to eat. Want to join me?

Freddy Frog: No thanks. I already ate.

Sammy Spider: (Sammy leaves)

Freddy Frog: (Sounding sad) I am bored, and I am looking for someone to play with. I can't play with Marvin Mouse because he's going to the zoo. I felt jealous. Then I saw Melody Turtle, and she made me mad because she was playing with someone else. Now I am sad, and I just feel like crying. (Begins to cry)

Suzie Frog: (Hears Freddy crying and goes to him) What's the matter, Freddy?

Freddy Frog: I'm so sad, and I just feel like crying.

Suzie Frog: Well Freddy, hearing you cry makes me sad, too. Now, I might cry. (Thinking, comes up with an idea) Hey, Freddy, I have a better idea. How about we sing a song. Sometimes that makes me feel better. (Suzie and Freddy begin to sing, sounding sad)

If you're happy and you know it,
Clap your hands.
If you're happy and you know it,
Clap your hands.
If you're happy and you know it,
Then your face will surely show it.
If you're happy and you know it,
Clap your hands.

Suzie Frog: How are you feeling now, Freddy?

Freddy Frog: I am not quite as sad anymore. Let's sing a little more.

(Suzie and Freddy continue to sing, perking up their voices)

If you're happy and you know it,

Jump up and down.

If you're happy and you know it,

Jump up and down.

If you're happy and you know it,

Then your face will surely show it.

If you're happy and you know it,

Jump up and down.

Freddy Frog: I am feeling very different now. I feel happy! I like the way I am feeling now. Let's go play!

Suzie Frog: Okay. Bye, everyone.

Feedback:

- How was Freddy feeling at the beginning?

- Where was Marvin Mouse going?

- How did that make Freddy feel?

- How did Freddy feel when Melody Turtle didn't want to play with him because she was playing with someone else?

- How did Freddy feel when Sammy was too busy to play because he was looking for bugs?

- What was Suzie Frog's idea to help cheer up Freddy?

- Does singing songs ever help to make you feel happier?

Watching for Winter

Characters: Boy puppet (Brian), and a girl puppet (Abby)

SCRIPT

(Brian in place alone)

Brian: (Looking up to the sky—he sighs impatiently) Sometimes it's hard to wait.

(Abby appears)

Abby: Hi, Brian, what are you doing?

Brian: Oh, hi Abby. I am waiting. I'm trying to be patient like Mom says, but that's hard sometimes.

Abby: What are you waiting for?

Brian: I'm waiting and watching for winter. The man on the TV says winter is coming tonight. So I guess I will just wait 'til it comes.

Abby: Brrr. It's cold out here.

Brian: Yes, that's one sign that tells us winter is on the way.

Abby: I love hot chocolate in the winter. Do you want some hot chocolate while you wait, Brian?

Brian: No thank you, Abby. I need to stay focused on my job here. I want to be the first person to see it when it comes. So I must keep a watchful eye.

Abby: There are a lot of things to do in the winter. What are you going to do when winter comes, Brian?

Brian: Well, I have been thinking about that. I will bundle up in my hat, boots, heavy coat and my scarf and go ice skating with my Dad. He makes sure it is very safe. We have so much fun, even though I get cold and wet.

Abby: (Abby giggles) Do you know what I like to do in the winter? I love to build a snowman with my friends. Sometimes we make them very funny. We might give him cookie eyes, and a banana for a mouth. I've noticed that a snowman can last a long time. Some melt fast.

Brian: Yes, that is a lot of fun. When we finish our snowman sometimes we have a snowball fight. That leaves us so cold and wet; we can't wait to go inside for hot chocolate.

29

Abby: I love winter. I wish it would hurry and come. I'll help you watch. (They both look upward)

Brian: Sally and her family are going skiing in the mountains this weekend. That's fun to do in the winter, too.

Abby: I guess we can't ski this weekend, but maybe when winter comes we could go sledding on Mr. Thompson's hill. That could be a blast, Brian.

Brian: Good idea, Abby. Hey, what's that?

Abby: What's what?

Brian: There's another one! (Pointing to falling snow)

Abby: I see it! Winter has come!

Brian and Abby: (Together, excitedly) It's snowing!

Brian: Let's get ready for our winter fun. Bye!

Feedback:

- What was Brian waiting for?

- What does Abby like to build with snow?

- What were Brian and his dad going to do?

- What was Sally's family going to do?

- What do you like to do in winter?

Signs of Spring

Characters: Freddy Frog, Suzie Frog, Sammy Spider, and Sassy Snake

SCRIPT

(Freddy Frog sitting alone)

Freddy Frog: (Sing to the tune of "Itsy Bitsy Spider")

The weather's getting warmer;

I love it when it's spring.

The birds begin to build their nests;

They really like to sing.

The baby animals arrive;

Flowers come alive

I love it in the springtime;

Give me a big high five.

Suzie Frog: (Appears, giggling) You are so silly, Freddy Frog. What are you so happy about?

Freddy Frog: I am just excited because it's spring. I can hardly wait 'til March every year because that's when spring comes. I love everything about it. Listen to the birds singing. They're building their nests so they can lay their eggs. The Mommy and Daddy birds take turns sitting on those nests, keeping the eggs warm. One day there is cracking and peeping. Out of the shells come those little baby birds. Mommy and Daddy feed them worms and bugs. It's not too long 'til one day those baby birds learn how to fly. Then they leave their nest and take care of themselves.

Suzie: I saw a robin this morning—and it had a worm hanging out of her mouth. She was going to feed her young ones. They must work hard.

Freddy: What do you like about spring, Suzie?

Suzie: Freddy, I like when the flowers come alive, then burst into pretty colors. The grass turns green, and the trees get new leaves.

(Sammy Spider arrives)

Sammy Spider: Hi, Suzy and Freddy. How are you both on this fine spring day?

Freddy Frog: We are fine, Sammy. We were just talking about how much we love springtime.

Sammy Spider: Me, too. I get to come out in the spring and begin to spin a silky web. That's how I catch small insects to eat.

I better get busy; it takes a while. Happy Spring!

(Sassy Snake slithers into scene)

Sassy Snake: Hi, guys. What are you talking about?

Suzie and Freddy: (Excitedly) Spring!

Freddie: We love all the exciting things that happen in spring.

Sassy Snake: I love spring. I crawl out of the rock I have been sleeping under all winter. I shed my old skin and I get new skin. I am on my way to lie in the sunshine. Bye.

Freddy Frog: Bye, Sassy Snake. You know what I like best about spring, Suzie?

Suzie Frog: What, Freddy?

Freddy Frog: The water in our pond gets warmer—let's go take a dive. Bye.

Feedback:

- What did Freddy Frog like about spring?

- What did Suzie Frog like about spring?

- What do the birds do in the spring?

- What did Sammy have to get busy doing?

- What happens to snakes in spring?

- What do you like best about spring?

Our Five Senses

Characters: Sally Sheep, Sunny Fish, Michael Moose, Freddy Frog, Father and Mother

SCRIPT

(Mother and Father alone)

Mother: Honey, it sure is a beautiful day today, isn't it? It makes you thankful to be alive.

Father: It sure does. Last night there was thunder and lightning and I heard it rain. But this morning we woke up and see the sun shining. Feel the warmth of the sun as it beats down on us.

Mother: Listen. Do you hear those birds singing? They seem very happy today, too. (Pause briefly) I love that sound. Look at the flowers. Don't they smell so good?

Father: They sure do.

Mother: Honey, do you want another slice of toast to eat?

Father: Do you know what I realized? We just used all five of our senses. We saw the sun. That is sight. We felt the warmth of the sun. That is touch. We heard the birds singing. That is hearing. We smelled the beautiful flowers. That is smell. Now we're going to have a slice of toast and that is taste.

Mother: Let's tell our friends!

Father and Mother: (Both call for Sally Sheep, Sunny Fish, Freddy Frog, and Michael Moose)

(They all appear as they hear their name)

Father: We're talking about our senses—seeing, hearing, smelling, tasting and touching. Let's play a game. Think about one of your senses, something that has to do with you. Then you will tell us what you thought of.

All: (All show agreement)

Sally Sheep: Baa. I'll go first. If you touch my wool, it feels funny. It feels different from Freddy's wool. That's touching.

Freddy Frog: (Laughing) I don't have wool, Freddy. I have skin and it's slimy, and it feels kind of rubbery. I have one; I croak really pretty. Some folks like to hear me croaking in the cool night air. That's hearing. Who's next?

Sunny Fish: My turn. When I glide through the water with my shimmery, shiny scales, the other fish say I look beautiful. That's sight.

Michael Moose: Good job, you guys! Sally Sheep's wool feels funny, Freddy Frog croaks and people like to hear it, and Sunny Fish is so beautiful, the other fish love to see it. That's three senses. Here's another one. When I am in the woods I smell the wonderful pine trees. They smell soooo good.

Father: You all really know your senses. But only four have been mentioned. We're still missing one.

Mother: Yes, that's taste, and I think we better go do it right now. I am hungry.

All: Yeah, Lunch. Let's go.

Feedback:

- How many senses are there?

- What are they?

- What did Sally Sheep say about her wool?

- Does Freddy Frog have wool?

- What does Freddy do that some people like?

- What did Sunny Fish say about herself?

Keep Our Earth Clean

Characters: Suzie Frog, Freddy Frog, Melody Turtle, Rhonda Robin, and Sunny Fish, Sammy Spider

SCRIPT

(Suzie Frog and Freddy Frog are seen—Melody Turtle sits quietly on the side)

Suzie Frog: (Sounding very sad) Oh, Freddy Frog, I am so sad.

Freddy Frog: (Concerned) Why Suzie?

Suzie frog: Because people have come to our pond and they have done something bad to it.

Freddy Frog: Oh Suzie, what could make you so sad? What did people do to our wonderful, beautiful pond?

Suzie Frog: They have put cans, and trash, and even broken glass in it. It no longer looks pretty. And it could hurt me and my friends.

Sunny Fish: Hi, Suzie and Freddie. I hope you don't mind, but I was listening to you. I am sad, too. There's so much litter in our pond; I can hardly see where I'm going. It's getting hard to breathe, too.

Suzie Frog: I have an idea! Maybe our friends out there could help us with this problem.

Freddy Frog: How, Suzie?

Suzie Frog: They can make sure that they never, ever throw trash in the water.

Melody Turtle: (Pokes out head) Or on our land.

Freddy Frog: Hi, Melody. Do you want to be sad with us?

Melody Turtle: I'd rather be happy. Let's be happy!

Suzie Frog: Okay, instead of sitting here complaining, Let's do something about it. Then maybe we will feel happy again.

(All show agreement)

Sammy Spider: I agree. I don't like it when our earth looks ugly. When people throw trash in our water and on our land that's called littering and causes pollution.

Melody Turtle: Yes, there's land pollution.

Freddy Frog: And water pollution.

Rhonda Robin: (Flies in) Don't forget air pollution. That is when people and businesses pollute our clean air. It gets contaminated, I know that's a big word, but it means it makes our air yucky. Then it becomes hard to breathe.

Suzie Frog: So there are several different types of pollution. There is land, water, and air pollution.

Freddy Frog: I believe our friends out there could really make a difference.

Suzie Frog: If they see people littering, they can remind them. They might say, "Please help keep our earth beautiful."

Melody Turtle: They could also recycle. That means taking their aluminum cans to a recycling place where they make new cans out of them. You can also recycle paper and other different things.

Suzie Frog: And with Mom's permission, maybe you can pick up litter someplace that really needs it. We all need to remember we can make a difference. Let's sing this song.

(To the tune of "London Bridge")

(All sing)

Pick up trash, and put in bins,

Put in bins, put in bins.

Pick up trash and put in bins,

Each and every day.

Let's keep our earth nice and green,

Remind our friends to keep it clean.

Let's keep our earth nice and green,

Each and every day.

Feedback:

- Why was Suzie Frog so sad?

- What could we say if we see someone littering?

- Can we make a difference?

- What can we do to help keep our earth beautiful?

- What does it mean to recycle?

- Name some things that can be recycled.

Being Thankful

Characters: Peggy Pig, Roger Rooster, Peter Pig, Cassie Cow, and Melody Turtle

SCRIPT

(Peggy Pig center, Roger Rooster seen at side listening)

Peggy Pig: One, two, three, four, five, six, seven, eight, nine, ten—Oh boy, there's just too many to count.

Roger Rooster: (He's been listening nearby) I can count too, Peggy Pig. Listen. One, two, three, four, five...

Peggy Pig: (Interrupts) No, no. I wasn't just counting for fun.

Roger Rooster: You weren't?

Peggy Pig: I was counting the things I have to be thankful for.

Roger Rooster: Oh, that is important. May I help you?

Peggy Pig: Sure, the first one is Mr. Peter Pig, of course.

45

Peter Pig: (Appears when he hears his name) Did I hear my name?

Peggy Pig: (Giggles) Yes, Mr. Pig. When I was counting the things I have to be thankful for, I said you.

Peter Pig: (Looking embarrassed) Well, thanks Peggy. I am thankful for you, too, and of course our nine little piglets.

Peggy Pig: That was going to be my next one. I am sooo thankful for my family.

Roger Rooster: Wow, you do have a lot to be thankful for. Is there anything else you can think of?

Peter Pig: Hmm, let me think. Oh I know, I am excited for my good friends, like you—Roger Rooster.

Melody Turtle: (Pops her head out of her shell) Hey, what about me?

Peggy Pig, Roger Rooster, and Peter Pig: (All agree) We're all thankful for you, Melody Turtle.

Melody Turtle: (Embarrassed) Gee, Thanks.

Peter Pig: Melody, Peggy Pig is counting the things she is thankful for and we are helping her.

Melody Turtle: I will help, too. Let's all think. (They all pause and appear to be thinking.) (After a short time Melody gets excited.) I know, I have one! I am thankful that I am healthy. Look how far I can stretch my neck out. (Stretch out her neck) I may be slow but I get around pretty well.

Peggy Pig: Good job, Melody. I need to stay healthy to keep up with those little piglets, so I eat a lot of vegetables, mostly corn, and I exercise.

Peter Pig: That's good, Peggy Pig, because I want you to live a long time. I just thought of another one. I am thankful for my home. Some pigs don't have a roof over their head.

Roger Rooster: And some chickens don't have a perch to rest on.

Cassie Cow: (Appears) Moo, Moo. Hi everyone. What's everybody doing?

Peggy Pig: We're counting things we are thankful for. And there seem to be many.

Cassie Cow: I have one. I am thankful for all my food. I eat a lot and I am thankful for all that hay, grass and grain. Moo.

Peter Pig and Peggy Pig: (Laughing) We are, too.

Joy Rothdiener

Peggy Pig: I've got another one. I am thankful for the sun and the rain because that's what makes all that food grow.

Cassie Cow: Moo. I agree with that.

Roger Rooster: I'm thankful for the air we breathe.

Peggy Pig: Wow, Roger Rooster. You're right. We wouldn't be alive if we didn't have air to breathe. So do you all see my problem? There are just too many things to count.

Melody Turtle: You know what I think? I think we should be thankful for these things every day.

(They all agree)

Peggy Pig: I have a song to sing about being thankful. Sing with me. (To the tune of "Frere Jacques")

(Each animal sings its own verse with all the animals singing together on the last verse.)

Peggy Pig: *I'm thankful for my family.*

And there is so much more.

Roger Rooster: *I'm thankful for my house,*

my perch, my door.

Cassie Cow: *I'm thankful for the rain and sun*

that makes our good food grow.

Everyone: *We're thankful for so many things.*

But now we need to go.

Everyone: Bye.

Feedback:

- What was Peggy Pig counting?

- What was the first thing Peggy Pig and Peter Pig said they were thankful for?

- Name the other things they mentioned the animals were thankful for?

- What are you thankful for?

Down On the Farm

Characters: Mother, Father, Cassie Cow, Peter Pig, Helen Hen, Rachel Rabbit, Donald Dog, Katie Cat, Melinda Horse and Sally Sheep

SCRIPT

(Mother and Father alone)

Mother: (Sounding tired) Charlie, I am sooo tired. I barely could crawl out of bed this morning. You know, living on a farm is hard work.

Father: Oh, it's not so bad.

Mother: That's what you think. Let's just think of a normal day on the farm and we will see.

Father: That's a good idea. First, I get up about 5:00 in the morning, to go milk Cassie Cow. That is very early; it's still dark outside.

(Cassie Cow appears)

Cassie Cow: Moo, Moo. I am glad you come on time. I give you a lot of milk. Then with that fine milk, you can make pudding, cheese, yogurt and ice cream. My milk tastes mighty fine over your cereal in the morning for breakfast. Doesn't it? Milk is good for your bones and muscles. It helps you to be strong and healthy. I better go. I have to eat more hay so I can make more milk. Moo. (Cassie Cow leaves)

Father: Sure is helpful to have ol' Cassie around. What's next?

Mother: Next, we go slop those pigs. That's pig-talk for feeding them.

(Peter Pig appears)

Peter Pig: Oink, Oink. Yes, don't forget about me. I need a lot of food. I eat and eat and then I eat more. I eat pretty much anything. I love corn. Then I lay around in the mud. People think it's yucky, but I like it. Thanks for taking good care of me. (Peter Pig leaves)

Father: Next, of course, are the chickens.

(Helen Hen appears)

Helen Hen: We hens work hard too. We lay eggs for you people. People eat a lot of eggs. You can boil them, fry them, and scramble them. You even color them at Easter. It's tough keeping up with such a demand.

Mother: We really appreciate your hard work. We enjoy your eggs. What's next? (Helen Hen leaves)

Father: Then, we go feed Melinda Horse.

(Melinda Horse appears)

Melinda Horse: Neigh, neigh. You give me oats and hay. I like green grass, too. I especially love it when you feed me an apple. Then you put a saddle on me and you put that nasty bit in my mouth. Icky. I don't like that thing in my mouth. But I give people rides all around the farm.

Mother: It sure is helpful to take Melinda Horse out to check on fencing when you need to, isn't it, honey.

Father: It sure is.

(Melinda Horse leaves)

Mother: What's after Melinda?

Father: Then I make my way to Sally Sheep.

(Sally Sheep appears)

Sally Sheep: Baa, baa. I am so glad to see you coming with that grain. I need to eat well. Sometimes you shear my wool.

In other words, you give me quite a haircut. (Giggles) People use my wool to make a warm coat, or a pair of socks, or a nice warm scarf.

Mother: Nothing like a good wool coat to keep you warm on those cold winter days. Thank you for sharing your wool with us, Sally Sheep. What's next, Father?

(Sally Sheep leaves)

Father: Then I take care of Rachel Rabbit.

(Rachel Rabbit appears)

Rachel Rabbit: Thanks for taking good care of me. I need food and fresh water every day. Then sometimes I give you baby bunnies.

(Dog appears, and interrupts by barking. Rachel Rabbit leaves)

Donald Dog: Woof, woof. Hey, don't forget me. Every farm needs a good farm dog. I help to round up the sheep and cows. I watch for strangers, too. When they come I do this. (Barking sounding a bit ferocious). I let everyone know what's going on. My job on a farm is very important. All farms need a good farm dog, like me.

(Katie Cat appears)

Katie Cat: (Gentle voice) Shh, Donald Dog. You are so loud. You are important, but so am I.

Donald Dog: You are?

Katie Cat: Yes, I make sure this farm isn't overrun with those pesky little mice. Meow, meow.

(Donald Dog and Katie Cat leave)

Mother: All of our animals are needed on the farm. They all have an important purpose.

Father: They sure do. I guess it's a big job just feeding and watering all the farm animals. Then when I am done feeding, I get on my tractor and head to the fields. I bale hay or plant corn, maybe even plow a field. There's always work to be done on a farm.

Mother: Yes, and when you're doing all that, I'm either working in the garden or in the house.

Father: You do work hard, too.

Mother: I am making pies, canning fruits, freezing vegetables, or cleaning house. And I always try to have a good home-cooked meal for you when you finally come in to eat supper—usually long after dark. I get tired just thinking of all the work we do on the farm.

Father: I guess you are right. We do work very hard. But it sure is rewarding. I really love the good farm life. Sing this song with me.

To the tune of "Mary Had a Little Lamb." (Each one appears as their verse is sung. They leave when verse is completed. Mother and Father sing first verse together, then leave.)

Mother and Father:

Farmers work very hard,

very hard, very hard.

Farmers work very hard;

each and every day.

Cassie Cow:

Cows give milk and say, "Moo, moo."

Say, "Moo, moo." Say, "Moo, moo."

Cows give milk and say, "Moo, moo,"

Each and every day.

Peter Pig:

Pigs eat and lay in mud all day,

mud all day, mud all day.

Pigs eat and lay in mud all day;

Each and every day.

Rachel Rabbit*:*

> Rabbits are very nice,
>
> very nice, very nice.
>
> We give lots of baby bunnies;
>
> Each and every day.

Melinda Horse:

> We are needed on the farm,
>
> We give rides, we give rides.
>
> We are needed on the farm,
>
> Each and every day.

Sally Sheep:

> Sheep get sheared, they use my wool,
>
> use my wool, use my wool;
>
> Sheep get sheared; they use my wool,
>
> Each and every day.

Helen Hen:

> Chickens look for food all day,
>
> Lay their eggs, look for food.
>
> Chickens look for food all day;
>
> Each and every day.

Donald Dog:

> Dogs are needed on the farm,
> On the farm, on the farm.
> Dogs are needed on the farm;
> Each and every day.

Katie Cat:

> The cats chase the mice away
> Run around and we play.
> The cats chase the mice away;
> Each and every day.

Feedback:

- Why was Mother tired?

- Name some things you can make with milk.

- What does Melinda Horse do on the farm?

- What do pigs do that some people might think is yucky?

- Why is it helpful to have chickens on a farm?

- What are some things that can be done with wool?

- What other work do farmers do?

- Do farmers work hard?

My Body

Characters: Boy Puppet (Brian) and Girl Puppet (Abby)

SCRIPT

Abby: I am going to the doctor today. Mom says, I am going to get a vaccination for a disease.

Brian: You are going to get a what for what?

Abby: A vaccination for a disease.

Brian: What is a vaccination and what is a disease?

Abby: A vaccination is a big word for an immunization.

Brian: That's not any easier to understand, Abby.

Abby: Okay. It's a shot, Brian. It's a shot to prevent you from getting certain diseases. That means sicknesses.

Brian: Oh, I think I already got a vaccin... (hesitates, unsure)

Abby: Vaccination, Brian. I know it's a big, complicated word. You know, our bodies are complicated, too.

Brian: What do you mean, Brian?

Abby: Well, when I say skeleton, what do you think of?

Brian: Halloween, of course.

Abby: Did you know that a skeleton is made up of hundreds of bones in our bodies?

Brian: Wow, that's a lot of bones. I know my mom tells me to keep my lungs healthy, what do you think she means?

Abby: When you breathe your lungs fill up with air. When you exhale you let the air out of your lungs.

Brian: Mom says I should never smoke, because smoking can damage my lungs.

Abby: That's right, Brian. I want healthy lungs so I am going to listen to her.

Brian: Me, too.

Abby: You know, it's important to have a healthy heart, too. The heart is a strong pump that moves the blood around in our bodies.

Brian: How can you have a healthy heart?

Abby: By eating heart-smart foods, like green vegetables and low-fat foods. And by staying away from too much junk food like chips and soda pop. Exercise is also important for a healthy heart.

Brian: I like to exercise, especially riding my bike.

Abby: Let's talk about other parts of our bodies. You name one and I will try to think of what it does?

Brian: Okay, my favorite is muscles.

Abby: Muscles help move your body. Your body has a lot of muscles and they are attached to your skeleton.

Brian: I know, I have big, healthy muscles, I am very strong.

Abby: (giggles) Yes, you are, Brian.

Brian: What about a stomach?

Abby: A stomach is a thick, stretchy bag that holds your food and helps to break it up after you eat.

Brian: Speaking of food, I am getting hungry.

Abby: Let's just do a couple more body parts.

Brian: Okay, Abby. I know a hard one. What does a liver do?

Abby: A liver is the largest organ in our bodies. Our liver cleans our blood and stores vitamins till our body needs them.

Brian: You are really smart, Abby. You must be using your brain.

Abby: Your brain is like a computer, helping us to think and do things.

Brian: Well, my brain is definitely telling me it's time to eat lunch. Let's go.

Abby: Okay. Bye everybody.

Feedback:

- What do our lungs do?

- How can we hurt our lungs?

- What can we do to have a healthy heart?

- What does a liver clean?

- What is a brain like?

- What was Brian's brain thinking he should do?

Ocean Fun

Characters: Boy Puppet (Brian) and Girl Puppet (Abby)

SCRIPT

Abby: Hi, Brian. What are you doing?

Brian: I am going to go to the beach today with my dad and mom. Mom said I could bring a friend with me—Do you want to come?

Abby: I love going to the ocean. What are you going to do at the beach?

Brian: There are many different things to do at the beach. But today, the first thing we are going to do is snorkel?

Abby: You are going to do what?

Brian: Snorkel, Abby.

Abby: How do you snorkel?

Brian: First, you put a mask on your face so you don't get salt water in your eyes. Then, you put a snorkel tube in your mouth. That tube will reach the air, so you can keep your face in the water and still breathe.

Abby: Is it scary, Brian?

Brian: No, Brian. I always wear my life jacket and stay close to Dad and Mom. It actually is exciting. It's amazing what you can see looking through that mask.

Abby: Like what?

Brian: Being under the ocean is soooo amazing, Abby. There is every color fish you can imagine. It's like swimming in an aquarium. Many of the fish are beautiful but some look funny. There is colorful coral where the smaller fish like to hide from bigger fish.

Abby: The ocean is really amazing. I have heard that you can be on a ship in the ocean and not see land or any other boats for weeks at a time. It's enormous!

Brian: Yes it is.

Abby: Have you ever seen an octopus?

Brian: No, but I saw a long eel once. It reminded me of a snake.

Abby: What about a shark, Brian. That would be scary.

Brian: Yes, it would, but there are many different types of sharks. Some are big and scary, but some are little and shy. Do you know what else I saw?

Abby: What, Brian?

Brian: I saw three flat stingrays resting on the ocean floor.

Abby: Were they big?

Brian: Sometimes stingrays can be very large. I just made sure I stayed away from the stinger in their tail. That could make me very sick.

Abby: Ouch, that would hurt. Sounds like you need to be cautious at the ocean.

Brian: Sure do. There are many dangers. You must be careful I would never want you to get hurt.

Abby: Okay, I will. But can we get going? I am excited. I want to snorkel and see all that neat sea life, then maybe we can build a sand castle on the beach.

Brian: I will go tell Mom to pack one more lunch for you, Abby. Let's get going.

Feedback:

- Where was Brian going?

- Name some things you can do at the beach.

- What is snorkeling?

- State some sea life you could see while snorkeling.

- Could the ocean be dangerous? How?

- When Brian and Abby got done snorkeling, what were they going to do?

Father

Mother

Abby

Brian

Polly Parrot

Baby Bird

Freddy Frog

Rhonda Robin

Helen Hen

Squeaky Squirrel

Katie Cat

Barbara Bear

Donald Dog

Melinda Horse

Sassy Snake

Suzie Frog

Sammy Spider

Melody Turtle

Marvin Mouse

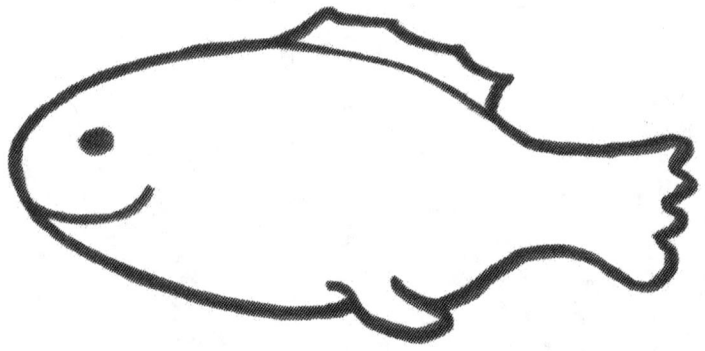

Sunny Fish

Sally Sheep

Rachel Rabbit

Michael Moose

Peggy Pig

Peter Pig

Roger Rooster

Cassie Cow

About the Author

Joy Rothdiener is lead teacher at Bolivar 1 Head Start in Bolivar, Missouri. She has been employed with OACAC Head Start for 12 years and been serving in the early childhood field for 14 years.

She and her husband, John have been happily married for 29 years. They have two wonderful sons and daughters-in-law. Joy loves to spend time with her two beautiful grandchildren—Kaylie and Braden.

Joy's favorite hobby is scrapbooking. She sees the importance of preserving memories for generations to come. She also has a love for music, which she uses in the classroom as well as her church.